1,003
Great Things
About
Teachers

1,003
Great Things
About
Teachers

Lisa Birnbach • Ann Hodgman • Patricia Marx

**Andrews McMeel
Publishing**

Kansas City

02 03 04 BIN 10 9 8 7 6 5 4 3 2

Library of Congress Cataloging-in-Publication Data

Birnbach, Lisa.
    1,003 great things about teachers / Lisa Birnbach, Ann Hodgman, Patricia Marx.
        p. cm.
    ISBN 0-7407-0989-5 (pbk.)
    1. Teachers—Miscellanea. 2. Teachers—Quotations. I. Title: One thousand three great things about teachers. II. Hodgman, Ann. III. Marx, Patricia (Patricia A.) IV. Title.

LB1775 .B52 2000
371.1—dc21

                                                    00-042040

Book design by Holly Camerlinck
Book composition by Steve Brooker at *Just Your Type*

--- **Attention: Schools and Businesses** ---

1,003
Great Things
About
Teachers

1,003 Great Things About Teachers

Teachers wouldn't be here if they
didn't like kids. (Right?)

All teachers vow that they're going to do
a better job than *their* teachers did.

Teachers can convert reluctant readers
into avid ones.

A teacher's jokes don't have to be funny.

They're allowed to walk through the halls
without a pass.

A teacher is great at saying "I can wait"
in an ominous voice.

Who's a better candidate for support hose?

They're good at spotting the
troublemakers fast.

Finding out a teacher's first name
is like spotting a rare bird.

Ready to disarm a knife-wielding
kindergartner at a moment's notice.

Teachers are sometimes willing to
assign TV as homework.

Great Things About Math Teachers

Can be used as lifelines on
Who Wants to Be a Millionaire.

Able to figure out how many square
feet of wallpaper a trapezoidal bedroom
with six oval windows will require.

On Parents' Night, they have
the satisfaction of knowing that
99 percent of the parents in attendance
know less about logarithms than their
eleventh-grade children.

If you are ever on a sinking ship
with them, they will be able to
tell you how much water you will
displace when the ship goes under.

Freely allow their students to
wield pointy compasses.

Know when it's respectable to use
a calculator and when it isn't.

Good to do overseas travel with—
can compute the dollar equivalent
of foreign currencies in their heads.

Happy to figure out the tip.

Good tax estimators.

Would have been totally prepared
if the metric system had been
adopted in the United States.

Really understand the difference between half and a third off.

Actually *use* the math their teachers always told them they'd need to know in adult life.

Are not fazed by negative numbers.

Could work in base eight
if they had to.

Never forget the difference
between a sine and a cosine.

Teachers are sometimes willing to discuss rock lyrics as literature.

They never let on that the last half hour of the day passes just as slowly for them as it does for you.

They know what to do in a fire.

A teacher can sing "Head and Shoulders, Knees and Toes" with real gusto.

If you teach young enough kids,
the really smart ones don't realize
they're smarter than you are.

Female teachers wear more colorful
blazers than female lawyers.

Able to memorize thirty-two names
(nicknames included) within the
first week of school.

Most teachers only have Bus Duty
a couple of weeks a year.

Great Things About Teachers— Real Kids Tell All

"They can make you be in a play."
—Henry, first grade

"They can make the homework easier."
—Tamara, first grade

"They care that you learn."
—Delia, second grade

"Mine believes that humans have
already been cloned."—Nick, fifth grade

"My mom is one."—Peter, first grade

"They dress fancy."
—Nicholas, preschool

"I love my teacher and I give him hugs."—Maisie, preschool

"They get to drive to school themselves, instead of taking a dumb bus."—Oliver, second grade

"They have good laps."
—Boco, first grade

"He's not too bad. Well, he's not
terrible."—Sara, tenth grade

"She taught us how to make a quilt."
—Jaime, seventh grade

"He fought in Vietnam."
—Slater, sixth grade

"He was at the first Woodstock."
—Sami, eighth grade

"My adviser has the coolest leather jeans!"—Dana, college freshman

"My teacher reads to us from *Winnie-the-Pooh* during rest time."
—Gregory, kindergartner

"I love my professor's accent."
—Lynn, college junior

"My teacher has really nice
penmanship."—Julia, third grade

"Our teacher's assistant looks
just like Britney Spears."
—Isabelle, first grade

"My teacher likes me."
—Roger, third grade

"He's not giving us
homework so we can watch
the World Series tonight."
—Sam, fourth grade

Unlike a child's peers, a teacher will never laugh if the child has an "accident" in class.

Be confident in the knowledge that if you have dandruff, your students will be sure to alert you.

Likewise, if your zipper is undone.

A teacher can quickly hem a skirt with masking tape if you fall and rip it.

In certain states, a teacher is not required
to know anything about evolution.

Teachers find Cliffs Notes as helpful
as you do.

Usually not portrayed as villains in
movies and books.

That apple on your desk is a great
source of fiber.

Words Teachers Are Not Embarrassed to Say in Public

Uranus

Bosom

Titular

Social intercourse

Fertile crescent

Penalize

Erect

Tentacles

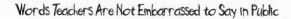

Frigate

Virginia

Bone

Rapier

Adulterate

Cockatoo

Consommé

Sects

Masticate

Balzac

Fallacious

Organism

Capitulate

Dickey

Crotchety

Screwdriver

Erroneous

Laity

Teachers get good at tolerating bad coffee.

If you're squeamish, there are good frog-dissection programs on the Internet.

Montessori teachers talk in nice, quiet voices.

Here's your chance to try (and discard) all your educational theories.

Teachers know what a dangling modifier is.

Falsely accused of a crime? Your teacher's attendance record can prove you innocent.

She cares, really cares, whether you know the capital of South Dakota.

Teachers never get lost trying to find the audiovisual room.

Allowed to raise their voices in the library.

Allowed to talk during a fire drill.

Student Myths About Teachers

Teachers never
go to the bathroom.

They're not allowed to have
their own children.

They're more sensitive to loud
music than "real" people are.

All teachers know each other,
no matter where in the world they live.

Teachers have a sixth sense about when
you are least prepared for a pop quiz.

It is impossible for a teacher
to get sick on exam day.

Your teacher talks to your parents
on the phone after you go to sleep.

In order to be a teacher, you must
be at least forty years old.

Teachers watch only PBS.

Teachers do not celebrate
their birthdays.

They never make mistakes.

They always make mistakes.

Teachers do not know the names
of any rock stars.

Some of them are escaped convicts.

Teachers were never students.

Teachers actually like fruit cup.

Free chalk!

Teachers have eyes in the back
of their heads.

Only a sixth-grade teacher knows the
difference between Vasco da Gama
and Ferdinand Magellan.

Be nice and your high school teacher
will write you a recommendation that
will get you into Dartmouth.

It's partly their fault when your
reading scores are low.

Your teacher-ID card gets you into
museums at a discount.

Library books overdue? No late fee!

Teachers get full-body shots in the yearbook.

They think the Pledge of Allegiance
is as dumb as you do.

Teachers' Tips: How to Spot a Forged Excuse Note

Smiley face next to signature.

Written in crayon . . .

. . . on paper torn out of
math workbook.

Student's temperature given
as 375 degrees.

Note is typed, with a mere
wobbly line as a signature.

Explains that "Catherine was so sick
yesterday that she almost died."

Signed "Owen's mother."

P.S. says, "Please do not mention my son's absence to me at the PTA meeting."

Student presenting the note is sunburned and wearing "Great Adventure" T-shirt.

If Peter's train leaves Cleveland traveling at 75 miles per hour and Susan's train leaves Los Angeles at the same time traveling at 92 miles per hour and Peter has four apples and $1.75 in quarters and Susan has three oranges and $2.40 in dimes, what is the answer? Only your math teacher knows.

They pretend to remember you when you come back to your high school ten years after graduation.

A first-grade teacher never holds her nose when you throw up on Stuart Perry's desk.

Kindergarten teachers have endless supplies of wide-lined paper.

They won't admit it, but they hate the vice principal as much as you do.

Elementary school teachers leap at any chance to have a party with cupcakes and juice.

Comedy writers have fed off nuns at Catholic schools for years.

Great Things About Swimming Teachers

They never quail at cold water.

They wear sensible swimwear.

Those good pool acoustics make them easy to hear.

They use poetic terms like
"flutter kick" and "butterfly stroke."

They're not afraid of the
high diving board.

They know all the good tricks
for getting you to put your face
into the water.

Unlike ordinary mortals,
they have plenty of kickboards.

They're not self-conscious about
poking their butts into the air
during a surface dive.

They can walk faster in flippers
than most people.

They don't care if their hair gets wet.

They don't care if boys see
them in a bathing suit.

Your teacher will never let the
school bully beat you up, at least in
the classroom, at least while she
doesn't have her back to the room.

The stricter you are, the more they
respect you.

Teachers really know their
Peter and the Wolf.

Nobody talks (or should) unless
you call on him.

Tom Hanks mentioned his teacher in his acceptance speech at the Academy Awards—and it could happen to you, too!

Society will always need teachers. Or so they say.

Teachers have heard all the knock-knock jokes.

They call talking "classroom participation" and give you credit for it.

Great Things About Being a Chemistry Teacher

You get the smart kids.

Other teachers don't understand
what you do.

You know that honey is no better
for people than sugar, because they
have the same chemical composition.

You can wear goggles.

Isn't it fun to pipette?

Only you are allowed to let your
students cause explosions.

Don't you love it when they discover another element to put on the Periodic Table?

Easy to get glycolic acid, the stuff that dermatologists use to give expensive facial peels.

Weird odors in your classroom have a perfectly good reason for being there.

You can bring home chemical models and tell your five-year-old they're Tinkertoys.

So what if you taught them something wrong? It'll be obsolete tomorrow.

A teacher wins coolness points by having a beard.

A teacher with a tattoo owns the school.

If you can draw well on a blackboard, you can draw well anywhere.

The thrill of control over all the blackboards in the classroom.

The power to grade those kids.

Think about it: have you ever seen a teacher with a run in her stocking?

At 3:00 promptly, you have a life.

And the malls stay open until 9:00.

Chaperoning dances used to be a drag . . . until you lost thirty-seven pounds and took that Dirty Dancing class at the local community college.

How to Be a Popular High School Teacher

Pizza, pizza, pizza.

Cry when discussing an affecting passage from "The Loneliness of the Long-Distance Runner."

Make fun of another teacher.

Bring in that newspaper clipping
of the time you got arrested in
that demonstration.

Use clips from TV shows
to teach history.

Show films of all Shakespeare plays.

"Don't ask, don't tell" policy regarding
homework assignments.

Students choose: midterm or not?

Complain about your own kids,
or your spouse.

Honor system rules!

Have lots of true-false tests instead of the "real" kind.

Hold classes outside.

Look the other way when students neck on the bus to field trips.

Ever hear of grade inflation?

Teachers get good seats at the
basketball game.

No one expects you to really *dress*
for class. Extra points if you do.

Make friends with this year's class mom.

Maybe this year's class mom will lend
you her ski house for a weekend.

Tell your kids over and over, "I passed the seventh grade the first time I took it, which is more than I can say for all of you!"

No one can decorate a room using cut-out magazine pictures, Scotch tape, and markers the way you can.

The opportunity to show off your (midwestern-accented) French. *Toujours!*

If you get married during the school year, you'll have loads and loads of flower girls, ushers, and handmade gifts.

Your own infant is the class mascot.

The high school students make decent baby-sitters.

No one expects you to defend Mary Kay Letourneau.

Great Things About Kindergarten Teachers

Liberal policy regarding gold stars.

Ditto on wearing mittens at recess.

Sometimes allow chocolate milk.

Always allow lots of marching time.

Tolerate Barney better than parents do.

Wear festive holiday-themed sweaters.

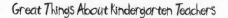

Can teach you how to skip.

Willing to shorten naptime
if there's a good reason.

Are allowed to use sharp scissors,
unlike their students.

Perfectly willing to help nine
thousand kids put on winter clothes.

Provide snacks that start with
P, W, or whatever other letter the
class is learning that week.

Teach you to plant seeds in eggshells.

Provide the last toy-filled classroom
you'll ever have.

Won't send you to the principal—
just to the time-out chair.

Can teach you such life skills
as tying your shoes, zipping your
jacket, and snapping your fingers.

Ta-da! Now that you're a teacher,
you're an instant role model.

It's still a thrill to announce a pop quiz.

You can direct the ninth-grade
production of *Antigone*.

There's always a teacher somewhere
in the building who's really, really
good at making costumes.

Teachers get to decide what's on the syllabus.

Montessori teachers let you call them
by their first names.

You can get one of your students to
bus your tray.

Visiting lecturers mean that
Happy Hour starts two hours earlier
and lasts an hour later.

Why Teachers Are Better Than Doctors

They do not give innocent little
children painful shots.

Do not require you to wear
a paper gown.

They don't have to go to med school
for eighty million years.

Use tongue depressors only
to make puppets.

Don't hit your knee
with that little hammer.

Better handwriting.

They don't tell you
you need to lose weight.

They never shine things into your ears.

It doesn't matter whether they have a good bedside manner.

A classroom is less contagious (sometimes) than a doctor's waiting room.

They're more willing to explain
the past participle.

More willing to answer questions
in general.

They don't suddenly yell out "Stat!"

Are our undergraduates getting older?
Or just looking more mature?

Amazing how you and your wife do
such an uncanny impersonation of
Richard Burton and Elizabeth Taylor in
Who's Afraid of Virginia Woolf?

Did you hate reading Joseph Conrad?
Boom. He's history. Never make your
students read him.

"My sophomores are smarter than your sophomores."

The bittersweet moment of middle school graduation.

You can tune your radio to NPR in the art studio.

If you don't introduce your seniors to Nina Simone, who will?

The Best Ways to Identify a Potential Teacher's Pet

Hand shoots into the air long before you finish asking the question.

Wears suit and tie or Sunday school dress on Class Picture Day.

Always ends book reports with
"The reason I loved this book
was because . . ."

Tofu salad and soy milk in lunchbox.

Comes up with independent projects
that are mere busywork, like listing
all the ways to total 5.

Mom writes teacher a lot of notes.

Dad asks teacher a lot of questions on Open House Night.

Parents videotape his/her every public appearance.

Allergic to peanuts—even just touching them.

You had Elisabeth Shue in one of your classes at Harvard.

You taught Amy Carter at Brown.

Your brother taught Steve Ballmer high school math.

Puff Daddy was in your gym class.

"*I* before *E* except after *C* or when sounded like *A* in *neighbor* and *weigh,* or the exceptions: 'Neither foreigner seized the weird heifer on the heights, Sheila.' "

The older the kids get, the less you have to see their parents in person.

Your students can still learn about manners from you.

What you can accomplish with just a glue stick and your imagination . . .

They are as happy about Friday as you are.

They are more afraid of the principal than you are.

Waldorf teachers know lots of myths and stuff.

Teachers are excellent spellers.

A teacher knows how to turn any body of knowledge into an outline.

Generic Report Card Comments—Work for Any Student!

"Could try harder."

"Needs to work on preparedness."

"Should pay more attention to the subject matter and less attention to her friends!"

"A pleasure to have in class."

"Please make sure parents sign all tests."

"Shows potential."

"Could participate more
in class discussions."

"Should check work more carefully."

"Always makes me smile."

Teachers know all the Roman numerals.

Despite what they say, they are as thrilled as you by the first snow of the year.

Only teachers know how to use cardigan sweater clips.

If you bring in your dog, your students will go crazy with joy.

Your teacher might let you take home the class turtle for the weekend.

A teacher's blackboard erases
much more easily than the kind
you can buy for "home use."

If the class turtle escapes, the teacher
probably won't get mad. In fact,
she will be secretly relieved.

They lend you milk money when
you forget yours.

The comfortable feeling of recognizing
the teacher's Friday outfit.

Report Comments It Would Be Better to Avoid

"This is the smartest child I've ever seen in all my years of teaching, even smarter than Mary Weinbach."

"At least he has nice clothes."

"Did not do a good job
when piercing my ears."

"I hate the little bastard."

"Living witness to the fact that
her parents have never
opened a book in their lives."

"His classmates shun him,
and rightly so."

"Who's Todd Garfinkel?
I don't think I've ever noticed him."

"This is a child without a future."

"I look forward to the day
we can be together . . . always."

Who else is going to teach you always to walk on the right side of the staircase?

Who else is going to teach you that you can practically go to jail for letting the American flag touch the classroom floor?

Who else knows how important it is to be line leader?

A teacher can always show you how to make book covers.

The thrill of seeing the teacher wheel
in a movie projector.

Those great moments when the teacher
says, "Let's put away our work. I'll just
read to you for the rest of the afternoon."

You can always tell when they're
yelling at you but trying not to laugh
at the same time.

They tend to have highly legible handwriting.

Things Teachers Know That Ordinary People Don't

Facts about the Industrial
Revolution besides the fact
that industry got started then.

When the Bill of Rights was written
(and exactly what it is).

What "factors" are.

How to make necklaces out
of gilded macaroni.

How to make papier-mâché.

The multiplication tables past the sixes.

When a haircut crosses that crucial
line of being "over the collar."

When a hemline crosses that crucial
line of being too short.

Who's already been line leader
this week.

More digits of pi than just 3.14.

How to run movie projectors.

The difference between the Mohawks
and the Algonquins.

How many yards are in a furlong.

Whether 2.2 pounds equals 1 kilo
or vice versa.

All the reasons for the Civil War
besides slavery.

What to say when a kid brings in Daddy's condoms for Show and Tell.

How to find the "star" inside an apple.

Seasonal classroom decorations:
snowflakes on the windowpanes,
construction-paper pumpkins over the
blackboard, a straw cornucopia on the
teacher's desk at Thanksgiving.

Seeing a teacher in the grocery store
reminds you that all humans share
basic needs.

Especially when you see toilet paper
in the teacher's shopping cart.

They let you have parties for all the major holidays. Also a few minor ones, like Arbor Day.

Some teachers will let you decorate your folders as part of the curriculum.

A teacher gives you ample opportunities to see whether his antiperspirant is working.

"What Do Teachers Do in the Teachers' Lounge?"—Real Kids' Answers

"Go to the bathroom, and sleep."

"Take off their shoes."

"Think of more rules."

"Chew the gum they take away from you."

"Practice trash-can basketball."

"Read kids' notes."

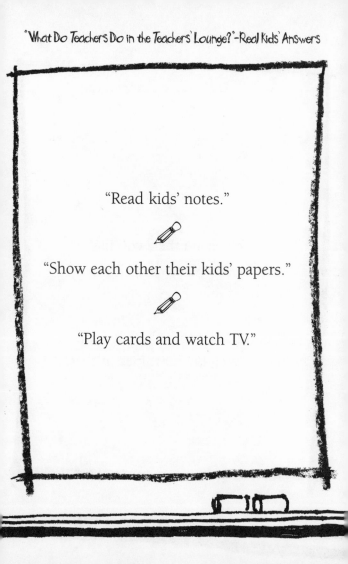

"Show each other their kids' papers."

"Play cards and watch TV."

"Drink wine."

"Tell each other who has
the worst kids."

"I haven't been inside, but I know
they have candy machines in there."

If there were no teachers, your mom
or dad would never have a chance
to be "room parent."

A substitute teacher really makes you
appreciate your real teacher.

They have a globe.

Your parents would *never* have been
able to teach you long division.

On Parents' Night, your teacher can usually be trusted not to tell your mom about that thing you did. (She'll save it for Parent-Teacher Conferences.)

They're not in it for the money.

What's the point of bringing your daughter to Take Your Daughters to Work Day?

The Best Teachers in History and Literature

Laura Ingalls Wilder

Annie Sullivan

Mr. Chips

Mr. Gruffyd in *How Green Was My Valley*

Mr. Mell in *David Copperfield*

The headmaster in
Tom Brown's Schooldays

Mr. Balanchine

Lee Strasberg

Miss Jean Brodie

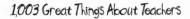

Ms. Frizzle

The shy, pretty one in
Up the Down Staircase

Vladimir Nabokov

"Sir"

Teachers are not afraid to get chalk
on their hands.

Teachers have very sensitive detectors in
the back of their heads that go off when
the class bully is picking on the class nerd.

Isn't it cute the way a teacher thinks
it's a treat to hold a class outside the
first sunny day of spring?

A teacher is very discreet about
his love life.

Seeing your effect on parents as they
nervously approach their parent-teacher
conference: it's still a thrill.

It is believed that teachers have no parents.

It is believed that teachers live in
the coat closet.

Great Things About Preschool Teachers

They're willing to change diapers.

They're phenomenal at ignoring
the bad breath of a roomful of
three-year-olds who haven't learned
how to brush their teeth.

They're fluent in toddlerspeak.

They know lots of clapping songs.

They know it's important to
equip the classroom with lots
of costumes and hats.

And speaking of costumes, they
know it's important for boys to be
able to put on dresses once in a while.

They let you bring your teddy bear.

They're not afraid of a little juice spill.

They let your mom stay if you're having a bad morning.

There's none of this claptrap about "early reading."

They patiently allow kids to
spread their own peanut butter
at snacktime.

The toilets in their bathrooms
are child-sized.

They're willing to read
The Story About Ping and
Caps for Sale countless times.

A hall pass signed by a teacher is better than a key to the city.

During a teacher's office hours, you may be able to get him to give you hints about what's on the exam.

A child's birthday celebration can use up at least an hour of the school day.

The New Yorker is full of cartoons that look great on a teacher's bulletin board.

A teacher will never tell you that you were bad in the school play.

They pretend to be pleased when you give them an apple.

Watch TV all night and blame it on your teacher. ("Miss Oslick wants us to study the effects of watching too much TV!")

Teachers have all the answers. Well, the textbook versions of all the answers.

Your teacher knows what really goes
on in the Teachers' Lounge.

Your own parents are afraid
of your teacher.

Give a teacher a blackboard and you
can count on him to turn around and
give you a spitball opportunity.

They know their way around the library.

Great Things About Being a Home-Schooler

Lunch is whenever *you* want it to be.

You're judge, jury, and executioner
all rolled into one.

It's easier to spot a kid
who's passing notes.

Excellent training in state regulations.

You can dispense
prescription medication.

The school day doesn't start
until you've finished loading
the dishwasher.

Taking your kids to the grocery store
counts as home economics.

No one can make you coach softball.

Your children will grow up in blissful
ignorance of what real children are like.

Full-year curriculum.

If your kids get into Yale,
it will make all the papers.

Teach in your pj's!

No need to metal-detect your students.

No need to waste paper on hall passes.

Kids can't tell you the dog
ate their homework, because
you don't own a dog.

Seeing a teacher outside school is a
big-deal celebrity sighting.

No one knows where teachers
keep their coats.

Teachers are never surprised
by a fire drill.

Why teachers always put pencils
behind their ears is an interesting
philosophical question.

The maintenance crew empties
the trash every night.

Summer vacations off.

Teachers get to work in an
asbestos-free building.

Nobody ever forgets their
first-grade teacher.

Why a Teacher Is Better Than a Parent

Doesn't care what time you go to bed.

Doesn't care whether you
brush your teeth.

Doesn't embarrass you in
front of your friends.

Doesn't talk about your posture
all the time.

Doesn't call you by your
older brother's name unless
she taught your older brother.

Doesn't have aged relatives
you have to visit.

Can't force you to write thank-you
notes to aged relatives.

Can't make you eat your peas.

Doesn't have your beeper number.

Won't nag you to feed the dog.

Won't keep telling you
your shirt is untucked.

Leaves you wondering
about his private life.

Hasn't seen you nude as a toddler.

Has no taking-away-TV-for-a-week
privileges.

Doesn't make you share
with your brother.

Never wears a bathrobe
in your presence.

Never asks, "What did you
do in school today?"

Only cares about one of your grades,
not your entire report card.

Out of your sight during holidays.

Can only bug you for a year.

Is not morally obligated to give you expensive birthday presents.

Doesn't check under your mattress for contraband.

Must ultimately answer to the principal.

Free parking.

Nobody stops a teacher from using the tennis courts after tennis-team practice.

At the very least, the school nurse has Tylenol.

Teachers' skin problems are closely monitored by their students.

The guidance counselor has all the
dirt on Lucy Mitowski.

Kids say the darnedest things.

The power to send someone
to the principal.

The power to keep you out of Yale.

Great Things About Debate Coaches

They're good with three-by-five cards.

They can instantly produce
valid opinions about any topic.

On debate days, they get you
out of school early.

What "fear of public speaking"?

They teach you to think on your feet.

They became teachers, not lawyers.

Even popular kids will lose
the tournament if their speech
doesn't contain enough evidence.

They always have something
positive to say.

They always have something
negative to say.

They know how to "project"
as well as any drama coach.

The power to wield a red marking pencil.

You handle the seating chart.

Confiscate toys to use as you wish.

So you got the date of the Magna Carta wrong. What fifth grader's going to know the difference?

Kids always look up to you since
you're the one standing.

Nobody can chew gum in your presence.

You can make small children
memorize long poems.

That smart aleck in the last row will
not be in your class next year.

All those children vying to be your pet.

Eat the extra cupcakes at
class birthday parties.

Not much to do during Assembly.

Likewise, book fairs.

Great Things About Being a Cooking Teacher

Your family will never
want for Texas Tommies.

You have unpaid child labor
to wash the dishes.

Tasting chili is easier than
grading final exams.

You know how to convert liters to
cups without looking at a chart.

You never have to buy lunch.

Excellent reason to subscribe to lots
of cozy women's magazines.

You can waste a lot of time teaching about the Food Pyramid.

You can explain exactly why the cafeteria lunches are so un-nutritious.

You have access to industrial-size containers of peanut butter and Swiss Miss.

Go ahead—have your daughter's wedding reception catered in the Home Ec kitchens.

Because you must set an example,
you always wash your hands before
beginning to cook.

On days you don't feel
like cooking, you can have
the students write meal plans.

You have a permanent built-in
excuse for being too tired
to cook at home.

Teachers don't have to take
the bus to school.

Workday over at 3:00 on the dot—
even if the job isn't.

Teachers can take a phone break,
and their students can't.

A teacher's desk drawers have locks.

Taking attendance kills
a couple of minutes.

Waldorf preschool teachers never have
trashy toys in the classroom. No plastic!
Wood, leather, and cloth only!

Teachers don't really have to pay
attention during Show and Tell.

Great Things About Gym Teachers

They refer to regular clothes
as "street clothes."

Unlike you, *they* are allowed to wear
"street shoes" on the gym floor.

They know every form of
dodgeball ever invented.

They always have a spring in their step.

They cancel games even when
it's only raining lightly.

Not that kids notice it, but they
tend to be in great shape.

They get to wear a whistle
and carry a clipboard.

They always, always know the
intramural game schedule.

They always, always know if the
ground is too wet for soccer practice.

They're genuinely patient as
long as you're really trying
to climb those ropes.

They teach you to hate bad
sportsmanship and cheating.

They have favorite teams,
and will discuss yours with you.

They understand the importance
of proper hydration.

They're a little bit scarier than
regular teachers.

They don't complain about
how hot it is teaching you
softball outside in June.

But they won't make you run
extra laps if it's *really* hot.

Give the kids a pop quiz and go drop
in on that cute seventh-grade social
studies teacher next door.

Teachers own big, solid,
refillable tape dispensers.

Teaching-supply stores.

Teachers don't get scared when
a bee flies into the room.

All teachers know how to touch-type.

Religious-education teachers
have a direct line to God.

Kids think it's a privilege to be
asked to erase the board.

Teachers get to wave a pointer around.

Great Things About Being a Driver's Ed Teacher

Nobody questions the relevance of what you teach.

Think of the simulated driving machines as video games!

Nobody knows left from
right the way you do.

It doesn't matter that you're
not driving the latest model.

No traffic situation can fluster you.

Driver's ed cars never seem
to run out of gas.

You always remember to check
your rearview mirror.

You know how far in advance
to turn on your blinker . . .

. . . and how closely to follow
another car on the expressway.
(One car length for each ten miles
per hour you're driving.)

You have access to lots of thrilling
movies about traffic accidents.

Go ahead and borrow the
class car on weekends.

Cops tend not to pull over cars with
signs that say "Student Driver."

You're the parallel-parking pro.

Where else will you get to drive
a car with two steering wheels
and two sets of brakes?

You never have to sit in the back seat.

Your students are desperate
to please you.

Funny student-driver stories come
in handy at dinner parties.

Kids respect cars *way* more
than algebra.

You don't have to teach your
students how to change a flat tire—
that's the parents' job.

When you're feeling down,
cheer yourself up by driving through
a row of orange cones *perfectly*.

She will ignore your dress-code
violations if it's the first time.

Teachers know all the good mnemonics:
Kings Play Chess On Fiber-Glass Stools,
Every Good Boy Deserves Favor, etc.

They're great at not noticing that the class
has planned them a surprise party.

All elementary school teachers know
the secret "Be quiet" hand signal.

Good handwriting covers
a multitude of sins.

Poor handwriting doesn't matter
if your ideas are good.

Mr. Frankel is remarkably convincing
when he says that tomorrow's test is only
measuring "how well you know the material."

They cheerfully accept the fact that their
classroom computers are totally obsolete.

Can recite the Pledge of Allegiance
convincingly every day for twenty-five years.

Great Things About Being a Guidance Counselor

You get to sit down all day.

License to pry into kids' personal lives.

No playground duty.

Private office . . .

. . . with a telephone.

Know the tricks to get your
own kid into Harvard.

Know which parents are too pushy.

Allegedly on the kids' side.

Didn't have to go to med school
to practice psychiatry.

Kids don't complain about the
grade you gave them.

You know exactly why Linda Mae
Appleton is "acting up."

You are legally required to report
any suspicious adult behavior
you hear about.

The American Cancer Society
will give you festive
antismoking posters for free.

Students like getting out of class
to see you.

When they go on strike,
you get to stay home!

More likely to have a first-aid kit on
the premises than your parents are.

First-grade teachers consider putting
your head down on your desk to be
an acceptable "rest."

They're not fazed by obnoxious parents.

When they get a cold, it's as good as listening to someone with a foreign accent.

Supernatural ability to hear someone whispering.

They never forget how to write a cursive *Q*.

Homeroom discussions can get as exciting as the opening segment of *Live with Regis and Kathie Lee*.

The Scents of School

Chalk dust in the afternoon.

Mimeographed handouts.

The girls' locker room.

As opposed to the boys' locker room.

Tempera paint in the art room.

Hot lights in the projector room.

Industrial-strength cheese sauce
on the macaroni.

Formaldehyde in the biology lab
(if you are of a certain age).

Steam tables in the cafeteria.

Anti-barf disinfectant powder.

Industrial floor wax.

Chlorine from the swimming pool.

The gym mats during a
wrestling tournament.

Cigarette smoke in the bathrooms.

Excessive amounts of CK One.

Teachers are easily impressed by multilingual parents.

Happy to accept ancient (yet working) computers donated by families for their kids' classrooms.

Boy, do they know how to punctuate.

Lots of colleagues to go to that reading conference in Plattsburgh with.

No one minds if a teacher's clothes are dripping with chalk dust.

They get to write on the blackboard whenever they want.

Teachers know how to make terrariums.

And they remember to water them, instead of letting them dry up.

Great Things About Art Teachers

Extrahuge vats of Elmer's glue.

Plenty of paste if you want a snack.

They have those good erasers
that don't make little shreds of
rubber all over your picture.

They can show you how to use
rubber cement the "real" way.

They have all the good colors
of construction paper.

Can show you how to draw a turkey
by using your hand as a template.

Your *mom's* not going to let
you sponge-paint.

They have scissors with cool edges
that cut weird shapes.

There are easy ways of drawing
trees, and art teachers can show
you what they are.

Unlike their students, they don't
draw peoples' arms too short.

They can be counted on to
wear unusual earrings.

They're allowed to use the paper cutter.

They'll come up with a project to
give your dad on Father's Day.

They know how to do papier-mâché around a balloon.

Olden-days art teachers used to make you copy, but nowadays ones don't.

They may have posters of famous naked statues on their walls!

Can make students feel privileged
just by asking them to pick something
up from the Xerox room.

What could be more fun than being the
one male teacher in an all-girls school?

What could be more exciting than
being the one female teacher in an
all-boys school?

Now that we understand about dyslexia, we know that little Rudy Sermer isn't *refusing* to learn how to read.

You can "guilt" parents with interesting jobs into making their office available for a field trip.

Free lunch.

Guaranteed parking every single workday.

You are not considered arch or coy
when you refer to your evenings
as "school nights."

No one expects you to spend much
money on your wardrobe.

Separate bathroom facilities
from the students'.

Does an ant have lungs? I don't know,
honey—ask your teacher.

Great Things About Music Teachers

They understand key changes.

They're never embarrassed to sing in front of other people.

They get to use a pitch pipe.

They can play piano with one hand
and conduct with the other.

They are (apparently) willing to
direct the fifth-grade production
of *The Pajama Game*.

Unembarrassed to jump around
like monkeys while conducting.

They preach the gospel of good diction.

Can hum a B-flat without
even thinking about it.

They aren't required to coach sports.

They understand the difference
between a major third and a
diminished fourth.

They know Christmas and Hanukkah
songs you've never *heard* of.

Can sometimes be conned into
letting you bring in a favorite
CD for "class discussion."

They have triangles and
other percussion instruments
just *begging* to be used.

They *care* about the difference
between ¾ and ⅝ time.

They know what *embouchure* means.

They understand the difference
between *andante* and *largo maestro*.

They actually have a favorite composer!

And teachers' bathroom signs say "Men" and "Women" instead of "Boys" and "Girls."

A chance to return to the place where you were long ago humiliated . . . this time with power.

A golden opportunity to blame everything on the football team/cheerleading squad.

Well, as an esteemed member of the
language faculty, you're finally popular.

Teachers keep the pipe-cleaner
industry alive.

They pretend to be fearless about bugs.

They respect the young so much, they
address them as "people."

Great Things About French Teachers

They never forget which verbs
are conjugated with *être*.

Some of those Balzac novels they
assign can get pretty racy.

French cuisine is considered a
valid part of the curriculum.

Language-study films are
surpassingly comical.

They know the difference between
Brie and Camembert.

Lovely photos of Mont-Saint-Michel
over the blackboard.

They want everyone to take
a junior year abroad.

They like to remind you how much
"freer" the American educational
system is than the French one.

No one else purses up their lips
in the right way when saying
"La mule a bu tant qu'elle a pu."

Every other year, they get to go
to Paris for free if they agree
to chaperone thirty-five horny,
excitable high schoolers.

A nice poster of *Jules et Jim*
in the classroom.

A chance to learn about *les vins.*

They're expected to be stricter than other teachers.

Madame Duhamel is *très* sexy.

Monsieur Lesjardins is a *vrai gentilhomme.*

Monsieur Thibaut *est ingénieur.*

Say what you like, Charles d'Orléans
was a great poet.

They know all the words to
"*La Marseillaise.*"

Even the president of the United States can't refuse a teacher the right to use the water fountain.

Even the president of the United States got yelled at by a teacher once.

Teachers are very good at making paper snowflakes.

Teachers can tell you whether George Washington or Abe Lincoln was a better president.

The clocks in teachers' classrooms are large and clear so that you can easily keep track of the seconds slowly ticking by.

Elementary school teachers know what you can't get away with in middle school.

High school teachers know what you can't get away with in college.

College teachers know you can get away with anything in life.

Great Things About College Professors

They always know which little bar
in town gets the first shipment
of the Beaujolais nouveau.

They're the big cheeses at graduation.

The reason they invented corduroy.

In a pinch, they can sub
for the chaplain during
morning prayer services.

They can actually make their
students weep while reading
The Odyssey in the original Greek.

Their wives get lots of exercise
lugging the baby's stroller up
three flights of stairs to their
charmingly bohemian apartment.

A pipe makes a nice affectation.

Donald Sutherland's the best
character in *Animal House*.

It's easy to be the "town eccentric"
on a small campus.

Willing (or at least required) to
teach endless sections of English 101.

They're so good at hiding
their extramarital affairs.

They don't get nervous when
they see little blue books.

They can get a table at the most popular restaurant in town . . . during the summer.

Helps if they enjoy amateur theatricals.

Can adjust to the lower cost of living on campus.

There are amazingly fascinating catalogs
for science teachers. Fetal pigs,
moth eggs, skeletons . . .

There are amazingly boring catalogs for
religious-education teachers. Maps of Bible
lands, "God loves you" stickers, wallet-sized
versions of the Ten Commandments . . .

Teachers know how to convert
Fahrenheit to centigrade.

A teacher who lives nearby can drive you home if there's early dismissal because of a snowstorm.

They know how to use a protractor.

They know the difference between igneous and sedimentary rock.

And they know why metamorphic rock is the strongest.

Teachers are the only people who
own staple removers.

Their skin contains tiny receptors that
can pick up the faint breeze of a note
being passed in the classroom.

Children will do anything for an A.

Nobody tells teachers to be quiet
in the library.

Great Things About Biology Teachers

Ability to use "reproductive" terms without cracking up.

Ability to explain the digestive system without cracking up.

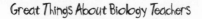

Know a fair amount of Latin.

Ability to look at the insides of a
worm without throwing up.

Know that creationism is dumb.

Can tell you exactly why leaves
change color in the fall.

Know what causes halitosis
better than any ad agency.

Care about global warming.

Sometimes have animals in the
classroom, or at least fish.

Don't get grossed out
during frog dissections.

But if you write a letter
explaining your feelings,
you don't have to do dissections.

At the science fair, will pretend
to admire your discovery that
plants grow slightly faster
when you talk to them.

Teachers know what's on your permanent record.

Only teachers actually know the difference between glue and mucilage.

Asking a kid to see if Mrs. Teicher is ready is like saying, "Would you like to play international spy for ten minutes?"

Lanyard necklaces with whistles and keys make wonderful accessories.

Likewise, brooches made of Play-Doh.

And pilgrim hats with turkeys stapled onto the front.

Books on tape make driving to and from school infinitely more pleasant.

Great Things About Substitute Teachers

They get that class is going to try to take advantage of them the first day they're there.

Since they don't have a huge stake in their students, they can sleep easy every night.

Might as well grade easily; helps them get requested more frequently.

Can teach what they want; they hadn't received syllabus in time.

They don't have to bother learning every name.

Subbing lets them put "teacher" on their résumé.

Just happy to be there.

Since kids are already prejudiced
against them, they can yell a lot.

Can squander lots of time pretending
they don't know where the supplies are.

When a kid objects, "But Mrs. Muller
doesn't do it that way," they get
to say, "Since Mrs. Muller isn't here,
we'll do things *my* way."

Mrs. Bailey has a Venus flytrap
in her classroom!

Teachers are the only people left
in the world who can scream
"Boys and girls!" without irony.

When an elementary school teacher
demands, "Are you talking to me?"
he or she is not quoting *Taxi Driver.*

Your high school social studies
teacher actually believes in you.

Mr. Norman hopes you'll try to be more
than a supermodel when you grow up.

If you're really, really patient with your
sixth graders, maybe you'll be beatified.

Your own singing voice sounds even better
next to the middle school chorus.

Great Ways to Distract Your Teacher

Pretend that the floor is heating up.

Ask about her childhood.

Ask about her cat or her kids.

Ask how this class would have been taught one hundred years ago.

Loudly whisper, "Did you bring the things for the surprise party?" just as class is starting.

Have everyone stare at the teacher's hemline so she will think her slip is showing.

Have everyone in the class
suddenly burst into song.

Earthquake! Suddenly throw yourself
onto the ground and writhe around.

Release a flock of turkeys or other
large game birds into your classroom.

Ask the teacher provocative
questions, such as:

—"How long would it take to
count to a million?"

—"How much did stuff cost
when you were growing up?"

—"Is it true that teachers used to
be stricter than they are now?"

—"If someone got sucked out of an airplane, would they be dead before they hit the ground because of the air pressure?"

Have a florist deliver roses to the teacher with a note signed "From A Secret Admirer."

Emit powerful eye-beams that will reach into your teacher's brain and scramble it like an egg.

You could have cast a tenth grader, but you do make a better Amanda in the school production of *The Glass Menagerie*.

Blanket excuses to take the class into the city to see any production of Shakespeare.

You can use the school's lamination machine to encase your driver's license and green card.

Only teachers know the difference
between oak tag and poster board.

Only teachers have the patience to
have a whole class make those
"handprint in clay" wall hangings.

It is more fun to smoke the cigarettes
you confiscated from your students
than to smoke your own.

For better or worse, you're a role model.

For better or worse, you'll be
remembered . . . for a long, long time.

You have an eleventh grader who's
already had a spread in *Vogue*.

You'll stay thin if you eat at
the school cafeteria.

Weird Advice Actually Given By Real Teachers

"Don't let your legs look like clothes hangers."

"Contact lenses are bad for your eyes."

"Pour water from a pitcher into a bucket to get a good B sound."

"Your daughter is learning to
read too fast—it will hurt her brain.
She should take up a hobby,
like spool knitting"
(said to the parents of a first-grader).

"Invest in a dinner ring when you're
older and get invited to dinner parties."

"Don't hitch a ride on the back
of a horse-drawn wagon—the driver's
whip might poke your eye out."

"Dilemma is spelled 'D-I-L-E-M-N-A.'"

"When boys quarrel, the best thing is for them to fight it out."

"Never read in bed—what if a bullet came through your window?"

"Never use the term 'rat fink.'"

"Learn to pronounce words correctly, or you'll end up as a high school dropout."

"Always cook with horse meat instead of beef—it tastes just the same, and it's cheaper."

"Don't be such a swaggering teenager" (said to a fourth grader).

"Single file, crocodile style."

You've already heard every
homework excuse in the book.

Since you never liked your high school
yearbook, you might as well be the
yearbook adviser and right an old wrong.

Teachers know that part of Russia is
in Europe and part of it is in Asia.

If you arrange "Smells Like Teen Spirit"
for the high school band, you might
just get away with it for Homecoming.

By now you know—really know—
Silas Marner backward and forward.

God bless Judy Blume.

You can borrow your students' cell phones
if you have an emergency at home.

Access to a bevy of eager-to-please
(or at least get an A) baby-sitters.

Great Things About Being a Private-School Teacher

In some states you don't need
to get certified.

Shorter school year than
public schools have.

Here's your chance to practice thrift, since your salary will be even smaller than that of a public-school teacher.

Rich students can entertain you with tales of their spring-break cruises.

You can be ultrastrict about enforcing the dress code when you're in a bad mood.

Since you have to sit with
the kids at lunch, you can work
on their table manners.

You can enforce shirt-tucking-in
and shoe-shining.

Kids can get expelled for
behaving badly.

Kids caught drinking get
a second chance.

You'll get invited to some unbelievable
bar and bat mitzvah parties.

You're allowed to call it an
"independent" school.

Maybe Timmy Lockhart's ambassador
father will speak at graduation!

Smaller class size.

Parents at a private school
really, really, really care how
their kids do in school.

You're known as a great lecturer.

Mr. Collins has a pet boa constrictor at home!

Your classes fill up before the semester begins (unless you teach at a college).

One word: tenure.

Wield fear.

You get questioned more by your
own kids in the two hours a day they
see you than by your students,
who are with you for six hours.

Uncanny ability to recognize
pupils from years ago.

Uncanny ability to be recognized
by pupils from years ago.

Great Things About Being a Writing Teacher

Just when you think you've seen
the worst poetry ever, something
new gets submitted that's even worse.

The job finances your real career
as a poet.

You have the inside track on all
those writers' workshops in Vermont.

It would be cruel to give anything
lower than a B minus.

You'll find out even more
than you want to know about
your students' sex lives.

Students' work sounds a lot better
when *you* read it aloud.

It's equally valid to require metered, rhyming poetry and free verse.

Feeling lazy? Have your students "analyze" one of your favorite authors.

Feeling lazier? Have your students read one of your favorite authors.

Feeling *even lazier*? Show the film
version of your favorite author's book.

Go ahead—make your students
read *Finnegans Wake*.

Published authors always remember
the name of their writing teacher.

Many, many, many copies of this book will be given to you each Christmas.

Ah, the pleasure of giving a low grade to a science project that was obviously done by a parent.

You don't have to tell the kids their history textbook is out of date.

You can teach your first graders that "when two vowels go out walking, the first one does the talking"—even though that rule breaks itself twice.

Teachers get Martin Luther King, Jr.'s birthday off in all states but Arizona.

Students may have to wear uniforms, but teachers never do.

Teachers have the power to dismiss early.

Teachers decide whether the classroom
windows should be open or shut.

Teachers don't get in the way during recess.

Teachers learn to rise above
the rough texture of those brown
institutional paper towels.

Great Things About Being an SAT Coach

You will *never* have students more eager to learn what you have to teach.

If you decide to go to law school, the LSATs will be a cinch.

You can have another day job.

But this is enough of a job that
you don't have to get another one
if you don't want to.

You have an unbelievable vocabulary
(of words no one ever uses).

Parents will pay you a lot of money
to tutor their kid on the side.

ETS's prestigious Princeton mailing
address sort of makes you an alum.

It's okay to swear in front
of your students.

You can wear whatever you want.

Play your cards right and you
can tutor a kid by the pool
of his summer house.

If you ever have to go
back to college . . .

You know lots of antonyms.

You know that "none of the above"
is usually the wrong answer.

You gain a healthy cynicism about the college-application process.

You tend to have a good supply of No. 2 pencils.

You absolutely know why "salt" is to "pepper" as "blank" is to "blank."

A teacher who wears a Halloween costume is perceived as a good sport.

They're pretty fair about displaying *all* their students' artwork.

They make up for those summer breaks by having to grade English papers on January 1.

Teachers don't get flustered on field trips unless one of the kids wanders into the forest.

Some teachers *volunteer* to take the
whole upper school to see *Les Miz.*

They're immune to blackboard squeaks.

It's funny to hear them try
to use current slang.

All those candles kids give you
for Christmas mean you'll be
prepared in case of a blackout.

Great Things About Drama Teachers

They would stage *Our Town* every
single year if they could.

Free makeup.

They don't mind as much as Broadway
directors would if Eileen Gaffney giggles
onstage in the middle of her soliloquy.

After the first performance,
the cast may give them flowers.

At cocktail parties, they can quote
from *Damn Yankees.*

There's always a possibility that
they just cast the next Julia Roberts
in Jefferson High's *Glass Menagerie.*

They know all about lighting, too!

Rapid on-the-job training
as a choreographer.

They don't have to memorize
anything; only the cast does.

Who knows? A Hollywood agent in the audience might discover them.

Never saw a production of
The Fantasticks they didn't love.

Not necessarily "into" grades.

So cool they allow students to call them by their first name.

Willing to rehearse kissing and hugging scenes with students.

Encourage the concept of "cast parties."

Allowed to swear during unwieldy rehearsals.

Sincerely believe rehearsals are more important than math tests.

Might not be "married"
in the conventional sense.

Think Stephen Sondheim is "God."

Refer to Liza Minnelli
as "the Goddess."

Someone to thank from the stage when you win your Grammy, Tony, Emmy, or Oscar. (If so inclined, make sure you don't out a teacher who is still in the closet, e.g., *In and Out*.)

Punish the cool kids!

Desktop publishing makes your job as literary magazine faculty adviser easier.

At last you have a date for the prom.

If you marry a teacher, you will
recognize that you have to be the
primary wage earner of the couple.

If you are a teacher, make sure
your life partner understands that
he or she will be the primary
wage earner of the couple.

Great Things About Teaching English as a Second Language

Learn to swear in different languages.

Learn many colorful foreign idioms.

Many of your students have truly inspirational life stories.

Some of the mistakes they make are really funny.

Tremendous satisfaction when your students get their first job using English.

The thrill that you get when
the student you taught five years ago
is an Intel Science Talent Search
semifinalist this year.

You can force students from "rival"
countries to talk to one another.

You get to point out that English
has lots of "foreign" words,
like *hamburger* and *spaghetti*.

H*Y*M*A*N K*A*P*L*A*N
was fictional.

You've mastered the arts of sari
tying and turban twisting.

You learn where to get the most
authentic Szechuan in town.

Now you understand why
kimchi is so beloved.

Teaching is a great second career
for dot-com billionaires looking to
"give something back."

They don't mind eating lunch
during second period.

They get to decide when it's snacktime.

They're doing God's work.

They are willing to be cops
all day long . . . and then they go
home to their own children.

They're genuinely interested in the
classroom's pet turtles, gerbils, bunny
rabbits, goldfish, snails, and so on.

And they're willing to take these
pets home during vacation if all the
kids are headed to Aspen and it's really
inconvenient to take the cage, bowl,
etc., on the private plane.

271

Adult Education—Why?

In order to understand
Woody Allen's jokes.

To get laid.

Your boyfriend's never going to
make those bookshelves he promised,
so you might as well learn how.

Hey, it's better than putting
your two-year-old to bed.

To finally learn to conquer your
fear of public speaking.

Because you could care less about
Monday Night Football.

To learn day trading.

It's easier to learn auto mechanics from
a stranger than from your husband.

If you take a "money" course,
the instructor will offer to set up
a portfolio for you.

If you only have one life to live,
why not learn the ancient art
of flower arranging?

Love to sing "Kumbaya" and "Puff the Magic Dragon" on any bus ride.

Feel the "Hokey Pokey" is underrated.

A day without taking attendance is like a day without sunshine.

Not discouraged from their profession
when metal detectors are installed
in the school entries.

Teachers feel genuine excitement
the umpteenth time they explain
mitochondria.

The volcano a teacher makes in
science class *always* erupts.

Bad Things About Teachers

Oh, sure, it's okay for *them* to come up with cruel nicknames for you and your classmates.

They can be sadistic on Friday afternoons when assigning homework.

They don't tell you they're pregnant until about the seventh month—even though everyone knows a lot earlier than that.

They don't seem to care about your infatuation with Frankie Munoz.

They don't seem to care about your infatuation with them.

They do seem to care about your lack of infatuation with Latin.

If your older sister was good at math,
they assume you're good at math too.

When they're calling attendance
on the first day of school, they
mispronounce a lot of kids' last names.

They remember every bad thing
you've ever done in school and almost
none of the good things, like the pep
rally you helped organize and how
you volunteered your mother to make
cookies for the Kosovo bake sale.

They believe that things they
did way, way back in the sixties
make them cool now.

Woefully insensitive to
this season's fashions.

Generally take your parents' side first.

Don't drive sports cars.

Even though they're scrupulous
at home, on field trips they're too
exhausted to care if students see
them smoking out of doors.

Someone to dunk in the water
at the annual school fair.

A reason to try psychotherapy.

Someone you learn *way*
too much about during the
junior trip to Washington, D.C.

No kidding, Mrs. Seymour
was a lawyer first?

Someone who can attend a
weekend-long seminar on the
new learning and enjoy it.

Teachers Aren't Fazed By

Body piercing

Indecent clothes

Ridiculous haircuts

Kids who sniff constantly
and never have a Kleenex

Sudden outbreaks of fake coughing
throughout the room

All the students dropping
their pencils at once

Rude language

Dog doo on a child's shoe

Inappropriate displays of affection
in the cafeteria

Ignorance

Throw-up

April Fool's Day

Crying

Six dead grandmothers offered up as
"I didn't do my homework" excuses

Dropped lines in the third-grade play

Finds storytelling with
puppets "relaxing."

Spends days off buying school supplies.

Someone had to teach
Dennis Rodman how to spell.

Mrs. McNeal loves the
Harry Potter books even more
than her fourth graders do.

They can write you the most intriguing college recommendation in the history of the Ivy League.

When you drive to your rival school for a mixed-chorus concert, you see the contents of their back seat and feel you know your music teacher in a new way.

When dangly earrings were in short supply at Bloomingdale's, the faculty lounge sported *dozens* of them.

Great Things About Being a Shop Teacher

Class too noisy for kids to talk.

The display case holding your students' work is much more interesting than the trophy cases down by the gym.

The coolest kid in
The Breakfast Club took shop.

Superbig classroom.

You know what a router is.

No midterms to grade.

You know which tools are too dangerous
for kids to use, and which aren't.

Admit it: you love using a power saw.

Admit it: you love being able
to produce big piles of sawdust that
someone else will have to clean up.

Students are proud of
their projects, no matter how
hard it is to tell what they are.

Make your own dining-room
table during your free period.

You don't have to call the janitor
when the window won't open.

Someone gets credit for teaching
Michael Jordan the jump shot.

They see that your acceptance to
college does reflect on them.

Sexy T.A.s.

Most senior faculty actually started
out as sexy T.A.'s—a long time ago.

If you're weird, most of your colleagues
will simply think of you as eccentric.

If you don't know how to work
the filmstrip projector, one of
the kids in your class will.

Teachers are less embarrassing
than your own parents.

Good Presents to Give Teachers

Gift certificates to restaurants
and bookstores

Gift certificates to teacher-supply stores

Tickets to Broadway shows

Donations in their name to education-related charities

Contributions to "Teachers' Discretionary Fund"

A fog machine (helpful in school plays and at Halloween)

Homemade cookies

Fine chocolates and other edibles

Teachers understand the subtleties of grammar that continue to elude you.

Can remember amazingly exhaustive passages of text. (How do they *do* it?)

Are unbelievably grateful to be invited to a student's home for dinner.

And then won't accept.

Teachers don't give too much
homework when it's Prom Week.

They know that deep down within
you are untapped reservoirs of genius.

Teachers are listed in the local phone book.

A.k.a. "educators."

Oh, don't worry about them.
They have a *great* pension.

Bad Presents to Give Teachers

Chalk

Fancy soap

Stoneware "teacher-themed" figurines

Plush "teacher-themed" teddy bears

Cheap jewelry
(unless handmade by the student)

Ashtrays

Framed pictures of your child

Their own report card,
thoughtfully written by you

Academic teachers are modest
about their athletic prowess.

Even if they're passing around
pictures they took on their vacation,
they'll never show the ones of them
wearing bathing suits.

Teachers don't wear
too much jewelry for daytime.

Though they work with construction
paper and glue, kindergarten teachers
are still white-collar workers.

Teachers are allowed to poke around
in their students' desks after school.

Teachers are less likely than most other
adults to cheat on their income taxes.

Just about no one else knows the
Dewey decimal system.

They rarely lose a child during
a field trip.

Great Quotes About Teachers

"You don't have to think too hard when you talk to a teacher."—J. D. Salinger

"Successful teachers are effective in spite of the psychological theories they suffer under."
—educational proverb

"Wisdom outweighs any wealth."
—Sophocles

"Since we are all likely to go astray, the reasonable thing is to learn from those who can teach."—Sophocles

"The art of teaching is the art of assisting discovery."—Mark Van Doren

"There is only one good, knowledge, and one evil, ignorance."—Socrates

"A teacher affects eternity;
no one can tell where his
influence stops."—Henry Adams

"The mediocre teacher tells. The
good teacher explains. The superior
teacher demonstrates. The great teacher
inspires."—William Arthur Ward

"Man is the only one that
knows nothing, that can learn
nothing without being taught."
—Pliny the Elder

"Learn the ABC of science before
you try to ascend to its summit."
—Ivan Petrovich Pavlov

"If I had a child who wanted to be
a teacher, I would bid him Godspeed
as if he were going to a war. For
indeed the war against prejudice,
greed and ignorance is eternal, and
those who dedicate themselves to it
give their lives no less because they
may live to see some fraction of the
battle won."—James Hilton

"In teaching it is the method
and not the content that is the
message . . . the drawing out, not the
pumping in."—Ashley Montagu

"Good teaching is one-fourth
preparation and three-fourths
theatre."—Gail Godwin

"The aim of education is to induce
the largest amount of neurosis that
the individual can bear without
cracking."—W. H. Auden

"The true teacher defends his pupils against his own personal influence. He inspires self-distrust. He guides their eyes from himself to the spirit that quickens him. He will have no disciple."—A. Bronson Alcott

"Teachers, who educate children, deserve more honor than parents, who merely gave them birth; for the latter provided mere life, while the former ensure a good life."—Aristotle

"A teacher is better than two books."
—German proverb

"A teacher who can arouse
a feeling for one single good
action; for one single good poem;
accomplishes more than he who
fills our memory with rows and
rows of natural objects; classified
with name and form."—Goethe

"To teach is to learn twice over."
—Joseph Joubert

"One good teacher in a lifetime may sometimes change a delinquent into a solid citizen."—Philip Wylie

"Headmasters have powers at their disposal with which Prime Ministers have never yet been invested."
—Winston Churchill

"The whole art of teaching is only the art of awakening the natural curiosity of young minds for the purpose of satisfying it afterwards."
—Anatole France

"Delightful task! to rear the tender thought,
To teach the young idea how to shoot."
—James Thomson

"The decent docent doesn't doze;
He teaches standing on his toes.
His student dassn't doze and does,
And that's what teaching is and was."
—David McCord

Teachers are not spoiled by
having an expense account.

They don't know any celebrities!
Isn't that refreshing?

They belong to a powerful union.

They go straight from a faculty meeting
to their own kids' soccer games
without breaking stride.

Teachers know the Latin and
Anglo-Saxon derivation of every
word in the English language.

They don't take it personally if
you fall asleep while they talk.

Business school professors earn less
than the students they once taught,
and yet they go on teaching.

How to Survive the School's Budget Cuts

Buy the giant economy-sized blackboards and cut them into individual classroom sizes.

Save on numbers! Eliminate 6–9.

Save on vowels! Who needs *Y* when two *Es* will work?

Generic teachers can teach any subject from chem to choir—and cost only pennies per class.

Imaginary field trips—even cheaper and more boring than the real thing!

Use birch bark for writing paper and tissues.

Fifty kids per class? Hey, it's a party!

So they cut algebra
from the curriculum?
Replace it with study hall.

Replace trigonometry with
silent thought.

Replace world history with
thinking hard.

Replace Spanish with just sitting there.

Have a schoolwide garage sale
for all the things no one uses,
like textbooks and the gym floor.

Save wear and tear on
your desk—stay home.

A good teacher is
part of you forever.

They know a lot more than you think.